GW00888634

Marian Green

The Book of Spells

II

Over 40 charms and magic spells
to increase your physical, mental
and spiritual well-being

SIMON & SCHUSTER
A VIACOM COMPANY

A QUARTO BOOK

Copyright © 2001 Quarto Publishing plc.

First published in Great Britain by
Simon and Schuster UK Ltd, 2001
A Viacom Company

Simon & Schuster UK Ltd
Africa House
64-78 Kingsway
London WC2B 6AH

A CIP catalogue record for this book
is available from the British Library

ISBN 0-7432-0777-7

QUAR.BEM

Conceived, designed, and produced by
Quarto Publishing plc
The Old Brewery
6 Blundell Street
London N7 9BH

Editors Steffanie Diamond Brown,
Tracie Lee Davis
Art Editor and Designer Julie Francis
Copy Editor Claire Waite
Photographer Will White
Stylist Lindsay Phillips
Illustrator Elsa Godfrey
Proofreader Pat Farrington
Indexer Pamela Ellis

Art Director Moira Clinch
Publisher Piers Spence

Manufactured by Regent Publishing
Services Ltd., Hong Kong
Printed by Midas
Printing Ltd., China

10 9 8 7 6 5 4 3 2

Contents

Contents

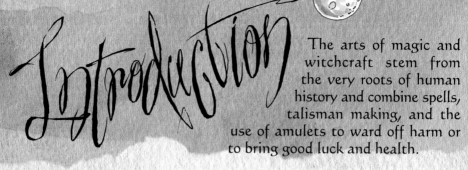

The arts of magic and witchcraft stem from the very roots of human history and combine spells, talisman making, and the use of amulets to ward off harm or to bring good luck and health.

The earliest written records include prayers and spells calling for help from the gods, healing potions, observations of the stars and descriptions of charms. This heritage would not have survived until today if it were useless. In modern times we understand the human mind better. We know that relaxation can assist creativity and that our dreams can reveal solutions to problems. Today's witchcraft, therefore, combines this knowledge with the ancient traditions to attract magic forces and make our wishes come true.

The Symbols of the Seven Ancient Planets

One set of symbols that is widely used in modern charm making and spellcasting is that of the seven ancient planets. Below is a list of each planet's associations.

ANCIENT PLANETS	DAYS	METALS	COLOURS	SCENTS
Sun	Sunday	Gold	Yellow	Frankincense
Moon	Monday	Silver	White/Violet	Jasmine
Mars	Tuesday	Iron	Red	Tobacco
Mercury	Wednesday	Quicksilver	Orange	Copal
Jupiter	Thursday	Tin	Blue	Cedar
Venus	Friday	Copper	Green	Rose
Saturn	Saturday	Lead	Black	Myrrh

The Tools of the Trade

It can be useful to look at the materials and techniques of ancient magic that are still used today. A spell is a collection of words, chanted, sung, or simply written, which asks for a specific kind of result. Spells are a simple form of magic, often used in conjunction with symbols and actions appropriate to the desired result or the god or power you are calling upon for help.

Talismans are made from precious jewels and valuable metals engraved with the words of spells. Incantations are chanted over them to empower them. Amulets are very ancient and used to protect a person or object. They are often shaped like an eye, to represent the eye of God that watches and protects. Charms are also physical objects, used to bring luck.

They are usually natural materials such as stones, plants or herbs that have medicinal and magical qualities. An appropriate material can be wrapped in a particular coloured silk to enhance its powers.

Using Symbols

The use of symbols with spells is the language by which we talk to the inner powers of our minds, to angels and gods who help us with our magic. Every tradition has symbols that need to be understood before they are used in spell weaving. Symbols, such as colours, scents and metals can relate to the desired effect of a spell, or to the power you are calling upon for assistance (see the chart below).

STONES	NUMBERS	ZODIAC SIGNS	ROMAN DEITIES	GREEK DEITIES
Diamond	6	Leo	Helios	Apollo
Moonstone	9	Cancer	Diana	Artemis
Bloodstone	5	Aries/Scorpio	Mars	Ares
Agate	8	Gemini/Virgo	Mercury	Hermes
Sapphire	4	Sagittarius/Pisces	Jupiter	Zeus
Emerald	7	Libra/Taurus	Venus	Aphrodite
Jet/Opal	3	Capricorn/Aquarius	Saturn	Chronos

Spellcasting

The spells described in this book are based on very ancient rules of colours, scents, numbers, materials and symbols, so each spell specifies the tools used to empower the spoken spell, such as coloured candles or ribbons and incense. It is therefore imperative that you follow the instructions carefully. To learn the original rules takes many years, so to ensure the safety and effectiveness of the charms and magical acts here, old spells have been simplified and modernised for today's spell weavers. Before you cast a spell, the following points must be taken into consideration, to ensure safety and success:

Colored candles

✭ Each spell must be thoroughly thought out and used only for a single, specific objective at any one time. If it harms no one you may work your spell, but you do have to discover what your true need is and then choose the best way of making it happen.

✭ Magic works for need not greed; it should bring you luck but will not bring you money.

✭ These chants will only affect the person saying the spell, as to try to influence another person, even for what seems to be a good reason, is dark magic.

✭ Spells only work if they are chanted with complete intent and focus. They are always very literal in their effect.

✭ Spell working uses the power of the trained and focused mind and can transform aspects of your life and the world around you, so make sure you are ready for change.

✷ Spells may be worked by one person alone, or by a group of friends or a family, but everyone must be in agreement as to their purpose.

✷ Once the spell has been cast the matter should be forgotten. It should be destroyed by fire and water once it has worked.

✷ Only work on one spell at a time, allowing between three days and a lunar month for some effect to be felt before going on to another.

✷ Much of this hidden knowledge is universal, so no matter where in the world you may be, it can be made to work.

Building a Base For Magic

Magic is a real force for change when applied properly. Just like electricity or gravity, it is difficult to explain or imagine, but anyone with a bit of patience and common sense can use it to alter the pattern of their lives. It is not necessary to believe in ancient gods and goddesses to make magic work, but you do need to keep an open mind, allowing yourself to accept that there are powers at work in the universe that can be helpful, without necessarily understanding how they work.

Most witches and magicians have their own ways of doing things. Their arts will have been built up through years of practice and the practical application of ancient methods to resolve the problems they face in their own lives and those of the people who consult them. To make these techniques safe and effective for people who don't have years of training behind them, the spells in this book have been simplified. Those of you with more experience will see how you can alter, enlarge and personalise these spells to make them fit your own level of expertise.

It is important that all newcomers to spell weaving practise the following basic skills to awaken their inner powers. These skills will greatly improve the effectiveness of your spellcasting.

11

Concentration

During spellcasting your focus should not be allowed to drift from the subject in hand. It is essential that you concentrate your mind pointedly on a particular subject, whether for a brief meditation or a long and complex spell. Complete concentration will help you send out a single, clear message to the powers that make spells work. A useful exercise to help you master the skill of concentration is to focus on the second hand of a watch or the changing digits of an electronic clock, for one or two minutes. This is a useful technique that can be practised while you are waiting for a train, for example, as most stations have a clock to concentrate on. It is, however, surprisingly difficult.

Meditation

Meditation is a method of communicating with the subconscious mind. It requires a relaxed body with an alert mind, and will only happen when you can deliberately shift levels of consciousness. Meditation encourages answers to questions, further information, or realisations to spring into your awareness. It is a passive state where these words and ideas arise spontaneously and it differs from visualisation.

Meditation

Sit upright and relax. Do not listen to music. Close your eyes and concentrate on your breathing, making it slow and deep. Allow a feeling of calm and relaxation to flow over you. Become still, letting all distractions disappear. You are in control and will remain so. When you feel ready, put the subject of the meditation—this may be a problem you need to solve, a word, symbol or piece of text—into your inner awareness. The idea must come ready formed to your mind. Allow a train of thought to develop around the basic concept, mentally noting the steps of its progress. If your ideas go off the subject, bring back your inner attention to the words or symbol and start again. Gradually, you will find that your flying ideas slow down, and new concepts focused around the subject of your meditation begin to attract your attention. Begin by practising meditation for just ten minutes at a time and allow this time to lengthen to a maximum of thirty minutes.

Creative Visualisation

An important part of magic is visualising the result you desire. This is an active process, again performed in an altered state of consciousness, when the body is relaxed but the mind is alert. It is best to ground yourself by sitting still, with your spine straight and your head held upright on a relaxed neck and shoulders. Keep your head up so that you can breathe deeply and easily and not slump. Focus on an image and build up a clear picture of, or, for people who find it hard to see, feelings about the subject. Create images in your imagination, describing such things as colours, shapes, atmosphere, landscapes and so on. Practical exercises include reading books that vividly describe scenes or actions in a way that makes you feel you are a witness, or participating in them.

A Note From the Author

I was fortunate to grow up in the countryside where there were many people who still used the traditional herbal and magical arts on themselves and their animals. From them I learned about the powers of the planets and plants, the elements of earth, water, fire and air, and many other things. The way that spells used

to be woven was always on a one-off basis, each situation being dealt with in a unique and individual way. To be able to do this, in the way it is written about in this book, is the result of over forty years of study, research and practice where I have been instructed by witches, magicians and wise country folk. These spells will work if you take them seriously and recognise that they are only a tiny part of a vast, ancient and magical tradition.

Creative visualisation

13

The Magic of You

A simple act of magic to illuminate your inner strengths.

You will need

A green candle

A recent photograph of yourself

Paper and a pen

A red envelope

Often inscribed over the entrances to various temples in ancient Greece, including the oracle at Delphi, was the phrase 'Know Thyself'. You can use this spell as a first step toward this process. By examining your own achievements and failures, which only you know, you can change your life for the better. This process requires a little patience and a lot of honesty, but it is well worth it.

Method

Light a green candle and, by its light, examine a recent photograph of yourself. Once you feel in touch with your image, take a piece of paper and fold it in half lengthwise. On the left-hand side of the paper, make a note of all the things you have always wanted to do and whether you have done them at this point or not. On the right-hand side of the paper, write a list of things at which you have failed and why.

When you feel the list is complete, tell your photograph how well you have done, despite your failures. Be positive. Select one unfulfilled ambition and promise yourself, solemnly, that you will take the first steps toward making it happen immediately. Pinch out the candle. Fold the list around the photograph, place them both in a red envelope and hide the envelope in a drawer for one month. Repeat this process often.

Going Within the Mind Map

Drawing a symbolic map of your life can result in a magical
pattern which will reveal valuable insights.

You will need

A map of your
home area

A clock or
watch

Two pens, each a
different colour

The places we call home are usually very dear to our
hearts, and often reflect an essential part of our very
beings. In this spell, a map of your home area is used as a
template upon which to draw a symbolic map of your life.
By plotting all the locations that play an important part
in your life and positioning yourself in the middle, you
can develop a better understanding of your place in the
world. This increased self-awareness can improve your
chances for success in life.

Method

Spread a map of your home area out onto a flat surface.
Spend exactly fifteen minutes drawing a pattern of your life
onto the map, symbolically marking places like your school,
your workplace and the homes of your family and friends.
Place yourself at the centre of the map and, using a coloured
pen, draw a line connecting each place to yourself.
Now plot out the places associated with people or situations
that you find difficult, or that cause anxiety in your life; use
a different coloured pen to connect yourself to these places.
When the fifteen minutes are up, stop and gaze upon the
drawing you have produced. Flashes of insight will occur;
use these as a guide to help you deal with the challenges
you face in your life.

Walking the Hidden Paths

In order for any spell to work, the spellcaster must be able to connect to the magical world. This connection can only be made when inner stillness is achieved.

You will need

*An incense stick
(any scent will do)*

A candle

Paper and a pen

Witches and spellcasters accept the existence of 'otherworlds', and know that these are the places where magic dwells. With the help of simple mental exercises, you can open up your mind and increase your sensitivity to these places. Such exercises require focus, patience and practice, but they are necessary for most people who wish to connect to the magical world. Here is a simple exercise to put you in a magical state of mind.

Method

Make sure that you won't be disturbed for about thirty minutes. Light an incense stick and a candle and sit upright in a chair, with your feet flat on the floor. Imagine the scent and light of the incense stick and candle enfolding you in silence and protection, forming an invisible sacred circle around you. Close your eyes and breathe slowly and deeply, concentrate on relaxing as you breathe out and focus on the rhythm of your breathing as you breathe in. Imagine yourself in your favourite outdoor location, until you feel you are really there. Feel the air, smell the scents, touch the ground and hear whatever sounds are most pleasurable to you in that place. A sense of calm will soon envelop you and a new magical world will come to open up before you. Open your eyes and jot down your impressions and feelings; these notes will help you achieve this sense of calm more quickly the next time you do this exercise.

Elemental Magic

CHAPTER
I

The elements of earth, water, fire, air, and spirit are used as a basis of most forms of magic and ritual. They are often associated with the four points of the compass, with spirit at the centre, although different magical traditions align the elements in their own ways. Each of the following spells uses elemental energies to bring about a change in areas of your life, so make sure you are ready for those changes.

Elementary Principles

Ancient and modern magic workers alike stress the importance of balancing the elements to give power to any spell weaving. The five elements each relate to a different aspect of life: Earth relates to the material world and practical things; water to emotions and feelings; fire to energy and enthusiasm; air to the intellect and ideas; and spirit to the indwelling power of life.

Representing the Elements

When working magic the elements of earth, water, fire and air are often placed at the edges of the magical circle to add their powers to the spells you weave. The following preparations help focus the mind and add energy to spells, but are not essential for the spells in this book.

To represent the earth element, stones, earth or even larger pieces of rock may be used. The water element is best represented by liquid from a natural spring or well, or rainwater, but bottled mineral water may also be used. Candles represent fire energy—and the force of the 'divine light' that helps the wished-for magic come into effect. As long as

The elements of fire, air, earth and water

they are housed in safe holders, any size or shape of candle may be used. Make sure candles are not positioned in a draught or where they can get knocked over and, if you burn them outdoors, put them in jars. The colour of candle mentioned in the spells is important, but a white candle placed in a red holder or on a red plate makes a substitute for a red candle, for example. Always snuff out candles before you leave the room.

The idea of burning incense to symbolise the air element is very old, for it was thought that the power of prayer or spells could be carried upwards in the smoke, to the realms of gods and angels. Incense can be found in many forms. Some edible herbs, such as rosemary, thyme or basil, have stems that can be dried to make incense and dried flowers of lavender, rose or jasmine may also be used. Incense sticks and cones are available in many scents. Some people prefer to use aromatic oils and a burner because it does not give off any smoke. Whichever you choose, test the incense before using it in a spell, since some people react badly to particular scents by coughing or sneezing.

Preparation is Key

Prepare fully before attempting to weave a spell. You need to choose candles and other items with care. Clear a space and set out any symbols you feel are necessary.

A magical circle

Create a magical circle in space and time by placing symbols of the elements at the points of the compass (see The Spirit of Sacred Space, page 32), This ritual helps you focus on the work ahead as it drives away distractions and unwanted energies.

The Element of Surprise

Magic doesn't always work in the way you expect, because it uses more than our familiar dimensions of time and space, so be prepared for surprises. However, anyone who has the perception to define an area of their current situation that could be improved will be able to use these spells and acts of magic to bring about beneficial transformations.

The Spell of the Earth

Magic is reliant upon the power of the four elements, and earth is the first of these. Earth is the element of grounding and stability.

You will need

A square piece of thick paper

A green, brown, or earth-coloured pen

Four pebbles or rocks taken from a natural setting, such as a garden, beach, or forest

A bulb or large seed, such as an acorn, sunflower, or pumpkin seed

Many of our goals and ambitions require a firm, solid foundation if they are to be completed successfully. Anything built upon an unsound base will only come crumbling down in time. This is not only true of projects at work or at home—it is also true of relationships of all kinds. This spell uses symbols representing the Earth to give the necessary grounding to your project or relationship, providing a stable, fertile place for it to grow.

Method

Ideally, this spell should be performed outdoors, but it will work indoors as well. Choose a project or a relationship that requires a strong foundation. Place a square piece of thick paper on the ground, if outside, or the floor, if inside, and write down your objective using green, brown, or any earth-coloured ink. Turn the paper over and, starting at the centre, begin to draw a tight, clockwise spiral using the coloured pen, until you reach the edge. As you draw, concentrate on your aim. Place one stone on each corner of the paper and put a bulb or large seed in the centre of the spiral. Imagine the seed growing along the spiral path. If you are having trouble conjuring up this image, ask Mother Nature to assist you. Once you have set the magic in motion, remove the stones and the seed and bury them in the ground. Fold the paper into a small square, hide it in a safe place, and await a favourable outcome.

The Magic of Water

Emotions, which are traditionally symbolised by water, play an essential role in making magic happen.

You will need

A green or blue cloth

A clear glass bowl

Natural water from a spring, spa, rain, or the sea

A compass

A few flower petals

In order for a spell to be successful, the emotions of the spellcaster must be open to receiving the energies of the spell. In other words, if you don't feel deeply about what you are trying to achieve when casting a spell, the spell will probably be unsuccessful. Water, which has long been associated with the emotions, can provide a means for you to connect to your deepest feelings, thereby opening yourself up to the power of the magic you are trying to access with the spell. By gazing into water, either contained in a bowl or in its natural environment, you can coax your emotions to the surface, and thus empower and enrich your magic.

Method

Spread a green or blue cloth on a table, and place a glass bowl in the centre. Pour some water into the bowl. Dip two fingers into the water and recognize that much of your own body is comprised of water. Touch your forehead with your wet fingers, then flick a few drops to the north, south, east, and west. Sprinkle some flower petals upon the water and watch them float. Focus on something you have positive feelings about, like the love of your family. Feel the full strength of these emotions; do not worry if they make you cry. Then say:

'From the love in my heart, I send out love to the world.'

After saying these words, you will feel a great release. Take the water outside and pour it into the ground.

The Being of Fire

A spell to help you energise and
empower every possible spell.

You will need

Your favorite
scented oil

A red candle

Whether in the form of a lighted candle, a bonfire or a
hearth fire, throughout history humanity has relied upon fire
to provide it with both energy and light. In the realm of
magic, the performance of rituals in darkness lit by firelight
can add enchantment to the work. Many spellmakers use
real fire to energise their spells, but it can be just as
effective—and safer—to use something flame-coloured
instead, such as golden flowers or fabric or a lamp with a
candle-shaped bulb. This spell calls upon the power of fire
to bring forth the energy to cast a successful spell.

Method

Work this spell in a draught-free room. Put a drop of scented
oil on your finger and move it up the length of the unlit candle,
working from the base toward the wick. Take care not to get oil
on the wick. Place the candle in a secure holder and say:

*'Living light in candle flame, let me give to you a name.
When I speak it, be my friend and answer with a shake or
bend. I call you (give the flame a name).'*

Light the candle and, when the flame is steady, speak to it,
using the name you have chosen. You may find that the flame
sways in response to the questions you pose. When you have
finished asking your questions, thank the flame and pinch it
out. Save the candle for the next time you wish to cast this
spell—the flame will speak again.

Air for Inspiration

A spell utilising the clarity of air to help you find the solution to a problem.

You will need

Paper and a pen

An incense
burner

Your favourite
scented oil

A small bell or
metal object that
gives off a clear
note when struck

A small fan
made of folded
blue paper

A feather

Scents and incense have been used for thousands of years in religious and magical rituals. Whether in the form of incense sticks or cones, real incense grains burned on charcoal or aromatherapy oils, a pleasant aroma can inspire clarity and enhance intuition and perception. Inextricably linked to the presence of an aroma is the act of breathing. When performing magic, rhythmic breathing can help develop the calmness and focus that are essential to spellmaking, especially if the air is pleasantly scented. Use this spell to summon forth the clarity of mind that you need to solve a problem that has been plaguing you.

Method

On a piece of paper, write down a problem you are currently facing. Place the paper underneath an incense burner containing your favourite scent. Now light the incense burner. Sit quietly, breathing deeply and slowly and allow yourself to relax. Breathe in for a count of four, then hold for four, breathe out for four and hold your breath out for four. Repeat ten times. Count as fast or as slowly as you need to, but always count evenly. When you are done, think about a problem in your life, and strike the bell or metal object. On that note sing 'help me' three times. Take a blue paper fan and gently waft the smoke from the burner away from you, watching the patterns it makes. A symbol of an answer will start to appear. Pass a feather through the smoke and carry it around with you until your problem has been solved.

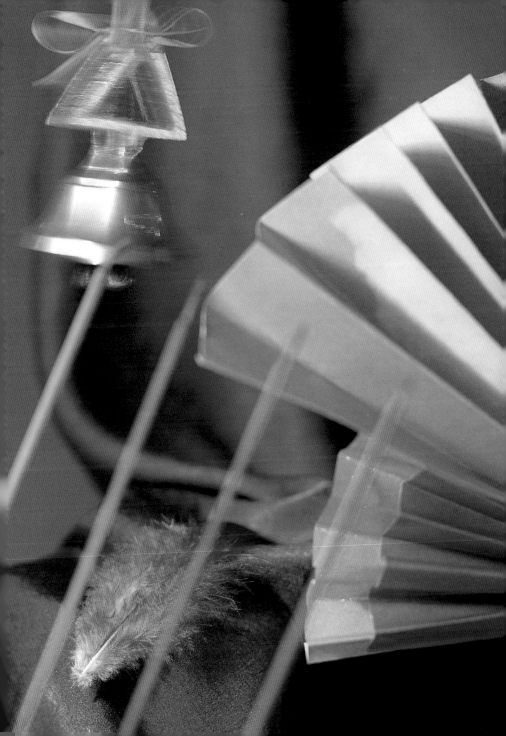

The Spirit of Sacred Space

The fifth element is that of the spirit, often symbolised by a lamp or a glass globe. To create a sacred space for working magic, it is necessary to find the spirit.

You will need

A green cloth

A compass

A stone
or pebble

A small bowl of
water

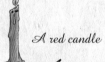

A red candle

Flowery incense
sticks

A clear glass
sphere (a marble
will do)

Using all of the elements—earth, water, fire, air and the spirit—this is a spell to help you to create a safe and effective 'sacred space', not just on Earth, but also in the magical realm, where the spirit of effective magic can surround you. When you reach such a place, your inner senses will open up and your spells will be empowered.

Method

Place a small table in the centre of your space and cover it with a green cloth. Using a compass to guide you, place the elemental symbols in position: the stone on the north side of the table; the water on the west; the lit candle on the south; and the lit incense sticks on the east. Place a glass sphere in the centre. Imagine the strong Earth supporting you; the flowing waters of the oceans blessing you; the flame protecting you; the swirls of smoke inspiring you; and the sphere of the spirit enlightening you. Place your hand on the stone and say:

*'I am a child of Earth,
but my destiny lies beyond the starry heavens.
I desire to enter the place beyond,
to work magic for the good of all.
So may this be.'*

When you have felt these forces, give thanks and let the experience fade away, putting aside the elemental symbols for the time being. A sacred space will have been created.

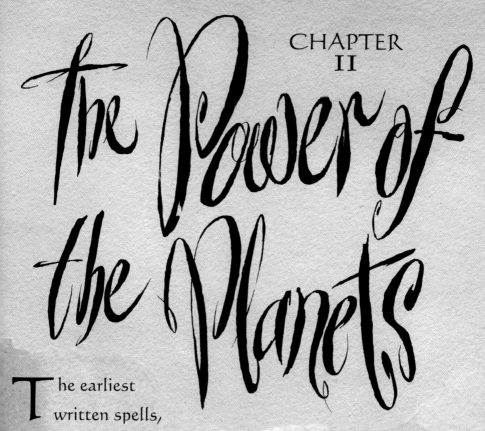

The Power of the Planets

The earliest written spells, going back 5,000 years, describe the energies attributed to the seven ancient planets and their use in magic and incantations. Each planet is linked to particular kinds of spell weaving and whether they are seen as personified gods and goddesses, or simply different energies, each one can help with a special area of our lives.

Calling on Planetary Help

The Sun, master of our solar system, forms a centre to our magic, the Moon inspires our visions, Mars brings energy, Mercury communicates, Venus offers harmony, Jupiter gives career enhancement and Saturn teaches patience. The more recently discovered planets, Uranus, Neptune and Pluto help with modern technologies and skills.

Old and New

The Sun, the Moon, Mercury, Venus, Mars, Jupiter and Saturn have been observed for thousands of years and colours, numbers, metals and influences attributed to each. Although not all these heavenly bodies are satellites of the Sun, from a magical point of view they are all called planets. Each of the 'old' planets has an effect on different aspects of life and magic through the use of symbols. The 'new' planets are also used and their effects are felt in newer pursuits including information technology, the nuclear industry, space research and the inner depths of psychology and mind power.

Heavenly Influences

Using the symbolism of each planet, including colours, scents and flowers, in a spell to assist its related area of life can bring great personal benefits. Natural materials, like wood, plants, stones or wool, work better than artificial substances. Threads used may be ordinary skeins of embroidery silk or wool, or sewing thread plaited into thicker strands. Ribbons may be narrow, wide or simply strips cut from a piece of material.

Each of the old planets is associated with a day of the week. The Sun is linked with Sundays when his enlightening rays are considered to be most magical, so Sunday is the most effective time to call upon his help. Monday is ruled by the psychic and visionary forces

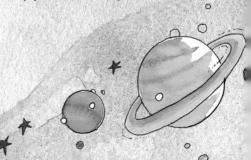

of the Moon. Tuesday comes under the protection of Mars, who helps with courage and determination. Wednesday is the domain of the great traveller, Mercury, and good for communication. Thursday is Jupiter's time, when commerce, career and material growth can be helped. Venus rules Fridays, bringing harmony, joy and love, and old Saturn, the grandfather of the planets, brings his slow and ancient wisdom to bear on Saturdays.

Understanding the Magic

I have been working with the powers of the planets for over forty years and found, through understanding their energies, often in conjunction with the goddesses and gods who share their names, that they really create change and bring wisdom. It is not necessary to believe in the ancient deities or to change your religious views to get spells to work, but to be open-minded and accept that there are powers in the universe that can help us in our daily lives is paramount. The power of each planet is indicated by the character

of its namesake, a god or goddess of ancient civilisations and each has something to offer the spellcaster as a filter of power and magic.

Although we know our Earth, with the other planets, orbits the Sun and the Moon is the Earth's satellite, in astrology the Earth is seen as the centre of the universe, with the Sun, Moon, and other planets circling it. Not only is the Earth the centre, but you are the centre too. From an esoteric point of view each person is the centre of the cosmos, and from that still point can request help, guidance or magical power from everything around. That help will be given, but there is always a price to pay, in terms of time and energy, dedication and respect, and eventually, thanksgiving for what is given.

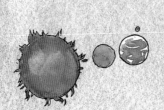

Planetary power

The Sun: Inspiring Inner Strength

A spell to enhance your self-confidence using the power of the Sun.

You will need

A sunny day

A gold
candle

A glass of
orange juice or
any other golden-
coloured drink

Each individual is the centre of his or her own universe,
much like the Sun is the centre of our planet's universe.
The source of life on Earth and an important part of
mythology, art and literature, the Sun is symbolic of our
ability to direct our will and to have a sense of purpose.
With the help of the Sun's light, you can increase your self-
confidence. This spell is best performed on a Sunday, when
the Sun's influence is strongest.

Method

On a sunny day, take a lit gold candle and a glass of orange
juice or any other golden-coloured drink out into the sunshine
(yellow and gold are sacred colours to the Sun). Hold the
candle between your hands. Close your eyes and feel the
warmth of the Sun shining on you. Sense the sunlight clearing
away any self-doubt and disappointments. Now lift up the
golden-coloured drink and allow the sunlight to shine on it
before drinking it. Say:

*'Power of Sun, force of light,
make my future strong and bright.'*

As you say these words, feel a powerful surge of inner strength
flowing into you. Keep the gold candle in your bedroom so that
you will be able to use its magical light and power whenever
you need encouragement in the future.

38

The Moon of Mystery

Drawing on the magic of the Moon, this spell will put
you in touch with your psychic side.

You will need

*A bright,
moonlit evening*

*A bouquet of
white flowers
including jasmine
if possible*

*A small round
mirror*

The face of the Moon has fascinated people for thousands
of years. Some of the earliest works of art are Moon-
shaped, with twenty-nine notches marking a lunar month.
The Moon's cyclical waxing and waning power influences
our dreams and moods and can also awaken our psychic
selves, whether her full white face or merely a slim, silver
crescent is visible. This spell is best performed on a
Monday, when the Moon's influence is most powerful.

Method

When the Moon is waxing bright in the sky, place a small
bouquet of scented white flowers (white is sacred to the
Moon) and a small round mirror on a windowsill. If possible,
include jasmine in the bouquet, as it is sacred to the Moon as
well. Standing in front of the windowsill and looking out at the
Moon, chant these ancient words:

*'O Moon of night, keeper of mystery, and bright stars' friend,
whose silver beams succeed the fires of day,
O three-formed Moon, who knows my dream,
come to me and awaken my inner sight.
So may this be.'*

Breathe on the mirror to make a mist, letting the moonlight
shine upon it. Soon you will see a face form in the mirror—
perhaps your own, perhaps that of a guiding spirit. In either
case, ask the face for insight, then give thanks three times.

Mercury: the Traveller ☿

A modern spell calling upon the powers of
Mercury to ensure a safe, trouble-free journey.

You will need

Sandalwood
incense

An incense burner

A small wheel
with spokes

Orange ribbon
or thread

A piece of orange
silk

Mercury, as he is known in Roman mythology, (or Hermes, in Greek mythology), is the ancient god of communication and travel. His powers are much in demand today, as we travel a great deal in our modern world—both for work and for leisure—and we often run into problems and delays. This spell can be used to help avoid such difficulties. Perform it on a Wednesday, the day sacred to Mercury.

Method

Place a small wheel with spokes and some orange ribbon or thread—orange is Mercury's magical colour—on a table. Light some sandalwood incense (sandalwood is the aroma dedicated to Mercury) and pass the wheel through the smoke, saying:

'Blowing air, have a care that I go safely everywhere.'

Now pass the ribbon through the smoke and begin to weave it through the wheel's spokes, saying:

*'Lord of travel, journeys' king, keep me safe when travelling.
Guard my home when I'm away, bring me safely back to stay.
Going forth and coming home, be my watcher when I roam.
In the name of Mercury, so may this be.'*

Repeat the words three times, then wrap the wheel in a piece of orange silk. Carry it with you whenever you travel for a safe, trouble-free journey.

Venus: Lady of Love

A spell to help you find true friendship or love.

You will need

Six green buttons

Green cord or wool

Fresh roses in a vase

Rose-scented oil

Venus is the Roman mythological goddess of fertility, love and pleasure (in Greek mythology she is known as Aphrodite). The great Roman emperor Julius Caesar claimed to be descended from her and introduced a cult dedicated to her. Today, Venus remains a symbol of love and romance. Her symbols include the dove and roses; her day is Friday. She will not make anyone fall in love against their will, but her power can be used to help you recognise those qualities that make you lovable. By appreciating these qualities in yourself, you can increase your power to attract others—both friends and lovers.

Method

On a Friday at sunrise, thread six green buttons onto a piece of green cord or wool (green is the sacred colour linked to Venus). Tie the ends of the cord or wool together to make a circle about five inches (13 cm) across. Pull out a few of your hairs and tie them into the circle. Place the circle around the bottom of a vase of fresh roses, picked from your own garden if possible. Pour a drop of rose-scented oil onto your hand, sniff it, and say:

'Lady of green, from high above, send to me the power to love.
With this circle here entire, send to me on wings of fire,
a vision from a heart confined, that to my worth I am not blind,
and so a true friend or love can I find.'

Allow a sense of your own goodness to emerge.

Mars: The All-Powerful

A spell calling upon Mars, the planet of courage, to help
overcome personal obstacles.

You will need

Scarlet felt

Red sewing
thread and a
needle

Five small iron
nails

Two red candles

Your favourite
incense

An incense
burner

A pinch of
tobacco

In Roman mythology, the planet Mars was associated with
war and thus great strength and courage was associated
with this planet. This spell calls upon these attributes for
help in overcoming personal obstacles and can be used to
end a conflict or to provide physical endurance.

Method

Using scarlet felt and red thread, sew together a bag strong
enough to hold five small iron nails. On a Tuesday (the day
sacred to Mars), stand two unlit red candles side by side. Burn
some incense, along with a pinch of tobacco (the plant sacred
to Mars). Pass the nails one by one through the smoke and say:

'Lord of iron, strength of steel, let your force my conflict heal.'

Place the nails in the bag and sew it shut. Light the left-hand
candle and say:

'Mars, empower me with your light, keep my courage shining
bright, that I may attain my right.'

Now light the right-hand candle and say:

'Mars, defend me with your might, give mental strength in
any fight, that I fear naught by day or night. Be it so.'

Hide the bag for five weeks. Your courage will keep you strong.

48

Jupiter: Lord of Justice

A spell to help you shine in the workplace and advance your career.

You will need

A square of royal blue paper

A pen with gold ink

•

Four royal blue candles in brass holders

Cedar incense

•

An incense burner

•

Blue silk

In Roman mythology, Jupiter is the father of all gods (in Greek mythology he is called Zeus). He is also the king of Heaven and Earth and is charged with the advancement of the solar system. In astrology, Jupiter relates to vocational success and represents growth and expansion. This spell can be used to gain Jupiter's support if you are experiencing problems at work or if you are seeking an advancement. It should be carried out on a Thursday, Jupiter's sacred day.

Method

Take a square of royal blue paper (royal blue is sacred to Jupiter) and a pen with gold ink, and write down a wish related to your work. Sign your name. Turn the paper over and copy this magical talisman dedicated to Jupiter onto the back.

4	14	15	1
9	7	6	12
5	11	10	8
16	2	3	13

Light four royal blue candles and place them in brass holders (brass is Jupiter's metal). Burn some cedar incense (the scent dedicated to Jupiter) and ask Jupiter for the help you need. Repeat this spell every Thursday for four weeks, and your wish will be granted. In the meantime, wrap the paper square in blue silk (to insulate its energy) and carry it with you.

Saturn: Lord of Time

A modern spell for time management,
patience and endurance.

You will need

Narrow black
ribbon

A black pen

White card

A coin

Scissors

A wristwatch

An ancient Roman deity, Saturn is depicted in black robes, carrying a scythe and an hourglass, for he is the lord of time. He can empower spells involving time and patience. In modern life, it can seem like there is never enough time to do all we wish to do. Not only is our time limited—our patience often is as well. This spell will help you manage your time better and will increase your patience, too. Cast it on a Saturday, when Saturn's influence is strongest.

Method

Buy a length of narrow black ribbon. Later that day, use a black pen to trace the shape of a coin onto a piece of white card. The circle should be no larger than the back of your wristwatch. On one side of the circle, draw the numbers of a clock face, but don't draw the hands. Cut the circle out and put it aside. Wind the ribbon around your watch strap and say:

'Mighty Saturn, lord of time, now I ask you hear my plea.
Let me learn to use the hours of the day most usefully.
Break the bonds that tie me down, teach me patience, day by day.
May your eyes of darkest brown smile on me along my way.
Minute by minute, hour by hour, bless me with your power.'

Repeat this mantra twice, then unwind and discard the ribbon. Affix the 'timeless' clock face to the back of your wristwatch and wear it every day, until the paper falls away or tears. The spell should take effect within the month.

Uranus: The Innovator

A planet of sudden transformation, Uranus's influence can be
called upon for a quick, decisive outcome.

You will need

Thin card

•

A pencil

•

Glue

•

Double-sided tape

Silver foil

•

Scissors

A safe sparkler
firework and
something to light
it with

First discovered by William Herschel in 1781, Uranus is
named for the Greek god of the heavens. Its magical
effects are linked to electronics, the nuclear industry
(which uses uranium), inventions and new scientific
discoveries. The power of Uranus can be called upon to
protect electronic equipment such as computers,
scanners, mobile phones, CD players and televisions from
power failure, viruses and other problems.

Method

Gather together all the electronic equipment that you wish
to protect. Draw the design of the *Ourobouros*, a snake with its
tail in its mouth, on some card as many times as you have
items to protect. Glue some silver foil onto the other side of
the card and carefully cut out each snake symbol. Arrange the
pieces of card in a circle, then light a sparkler. Draw a serpent
in the air with the sparkler above each of the symbols and ask
Uranus, in your own words, to bless and protect all of your
electronic equipment. When the sparkler has gone out, using
double-sided tape stick the snake symbols onto the back of
each item to be protected, placing them so they can't be
seen. Do not tell anyone that you have performed this spell
or it will not work.

Neptune: Bringer of Sight

A spell calling upon the power of the distant planet Neptune to awaken your psychic visionary sense and give you the power to 'see'.

You will need

A seashell
(optional)

A clear glass
bowl of water

Table salt

In Roman mythology, the god Neptune rules the seas, all of the creatures within them and the tides (in Greek mythology he is called Poseidon). With the help of his subtle energies, you can use this spell to activate your hidden psychic abilities. This force needs to be carefully controlled, however, so that, like a large wave, it doesn't overwhelm you.

Method

Place a glass bowl of water in front of you and add a few pinches of salt. If you have a real seashell, place it in the bowl of water. Now say:

'Become as the great sea, realm of Neptune, cradle of life. As your water is clear, so may my vision be clear.'

Sit quietly with your eyes closed. Breathe deeply and slowly and start to relax. Breathe in for a count of four, hold it for four, then breathe out for four and hold for four. Repeat this exercise ten times. Imagine that your feet and legs are black, linking you to the Earth, and that your lap is scarlet, your belly orange, your solar plexus yellow, and your heart region green. See your throat as blue, your forehead as purple, and above your head, linking you to Heaven, a ball of brilliant white fire. With this image in your mind, gaze into the water. If you are sufficiently relaxed and attuned, Neptune will grant you a vision. Whether or not you receive a vision, thank the power of Neptune.

Pluto: The Keeper of Memories

A spell to summon forth the ancient power
of Pluto to convene with your ancestors.

You will need

*A mirror on a
stand*

•

A white candle

*A copy of your
family tree or
other memento of
the past*

•

*Sweet, smoky
incense*

•

*An incense
burner*

•

Paper and pen

The planet Pluto was named after the Roman god of the underworld (also called Pluto). The mythical underworld is often associated with a psychological phenomenon known as the collective unconscious, where ancient ancestral memories are stored. This spell calls upon Pluto's power to connect you with your ancestors. Perform this spell at night.

Method

Make a magical circle of protection and calmness by blessing some water (using your own words) and sprinkling it around you. Place a mirror on a stand, light a white candle and place them both on a table, so that the light shines onto the mirror. Lay your family tree, or some other memento from your past, on the table and burn some incense. Write on a piece of paper:

'I wish to remember my ancestors, and those from my family who I have forgotten about. Reveal to me in this shining glass, I summon kind memories of my old family by this powerful spell.'

Carefully burn the paper in the candle flame, focusing your vision on the smoke reflected in the mirror. A face may appear in the mirror. When the image has faded, say:

*'Thank you, whoever you seem,
perhaps we will meet again in a dream.'*

You may meet a family member or an ancestor in your dreams.

56

Sealed spell

A Cosmos Spell

A talisman to bring you the luck of the planets.

You will need

(The materials below should relate to the planet you have chosen for this spell)

A number of
coloured candles

•

Coloured paper

•

Coloured silk

•

Scissors

•

A felt-tip pen

•

A small metal
object

Each planet rules over its own special domain and thus each can be asked for help in a different area. Ancient talismans were typically written on animal skins using special inks, or were made of metal and jewels, but modern ones can be made using coloured paper and felt-tip pens. Below, you will find a list of the planets, along with their associated powers, colors, metals, numbers and days of the week. Decide which planet best represents the luck you need and summon it forth with the help of this spell.

ANCIENT PLANETS	DAYS	METALS
Sun	Sunday	Gold
Moon	Monday	Silver
Mars	Tuesday	Iron
Mercury	Wednesday	Quicksilver
Jupiter	Thursday	Tin
Venus	Friday	Copper
Saturn	Saturday	Lead

Method

On your chosen planet's day, collect the appropriate number of candles, some paper, a pen and a piece of silk, all in the planet's colour. Find something made of the metal dedicated to the planet. Cut the paper into a shape with the appropriate number of sides, then write down the luck you need. Light the candles, place the metal object on the paper, and visualise yourself getting the help you need. Snuff out the candles and wrap the paper in the silk, to protect its energy. Carry this package around for two weeks. Your luck will come.

The Symbols of The Seven Ancient Planets
One set of symbols that is widely used in modern charm making and spellcasting is that of the seven ancient planets and their corresponding days, metals, colours, numbers and powers.

COLOURS	NUMBERS	POWERS
Yellow	6	Health
White/violet	9	Psychic skills
Red	5	Courage
Orange	8	Communication
Blue	4	Expansion
Green	7	Harmony
Black	3	Patience

The Magic of time

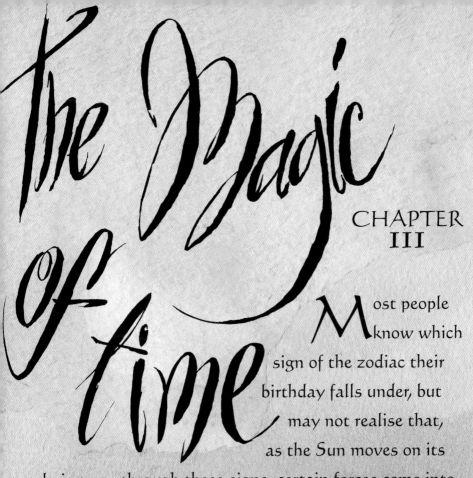

CHAPTER
III

Most people know which sign of the zodiac their birthday falls under, but may not realise that, as the Sun moves on its yearly journey through these signs, certain forces come into operation. Our earliest ancestors, who watched the movements of the lights in the sky, mapped out these periods of time and the energies, benefits and difficulties each offered. This knowledge has been expanded and explored, so that now, as each sign of the zodiac rules the skies, anyone who wishes may make use of these forces in their own lives.

Time's Influence on Magic

Much magic is concerned with time, choosing the right hour, day, month or season to bring about special forms of luck, progress, self-assurance or success. Magic workers associate certain kinds of spells, rituals and celebrations with particular times of the year.

The Zodiac Timepiece

The signs of the zodiac form a circular wall of stars that surrounds us, with the Earth at the centre of the circle. The exact movements of the planets within the signs of the zodiac are recorded in tables called *Ephemeris*, either in a book or on the Internet.

The different constellations of the zodiac can be seen as numbers on the face of a great cosmic clock. Unlike our time clocks, the zodiac clock has one hand for each of the planets, all moving at different speeds around the dial. In a person's horoscope, the settings of all these hands is recorded at the moment of birth, when the position of every sign and planet has a significance. Our birthplace forms the central point around which these many

influences move, faster or slower, throughout our lives, influencing everything we do.

To use the zodiacal influences in magic, we only need to weave spells that call upon each of the sign's specific powers. For simple spells you need to know when each sign of the zodiac has its greatest influence. Because of

Aries	March 21 to April 19	
Taurus	April 20 to May 20	
Gemini	May 21 to June 21	midsummer solstice
Cancer	June 22 to July 22	
Leo	July 23 to August 22	
Virgo	August 23 to Sept 22	autumn equinox
Libra	Sept 23 to Oct 22	
Scorpio	Oct 23 to Nov 21	
Sagittarius	Nov 22 to Dec 21	winter solstice
Capricorn	Dec 22 to Jan 19	
Aquarius	Jan 20 to Feb 18	
Pisces	Feb 19 to March 20	spring equinox

the wobble of the Earth against the stars, exact dates may vary from year to year, by a day or two. Astrological information given in newspapers or on the Internet will tell you what is happening in a particular year.

Symbols in the Stars

Records of certain fixed patterns of stars, called constellations, were observed and named by the wise peoples in many lands, especially those with dry climates, where the skies are usually clear for most of the year. In each land these constellations were seen as vast figures of people or things and given names. Stories were told about the great heroes of the zodiac, Castor and Pollux, the twins of Gemini, Leo the lion, or Sagittarius, the celestial archer. No one knows which came first, the myth or the huge starry figures' adventures. Sometimes the heroine of an old tale fell in love with an immortal god and, as a gift, was given eternal life and turned into a star. In ancient Egypt the god Osiris is shown by the constellation we know as

Zodiac symbols represent the fixed patterns of stars

Orion, and Isis, his wife, is shown by Sirius, the brightest star in the sky, which follows on the heels of Orion.

Early astronomers believed that children born when certain stars were visible grew up to show particular qualities. Recent research by Michel Gauqueline, looking at the horoscopes of soldiers, artists, doctors and sports figures, found that the position of certain planets in their charts were similar.

The following zodiac spells can be used for many purposes, in order to bring balance in a relationship or justice to the world, or protection to a place or person, for example. The chart on pages 8–9 describes which zodiac signs are powerful on each day of the week. If you live in the southern hemisphere the zodiac signs from Gemini to Virgo are in the winter, so you will need to take this into account when spell weaving. If roses don't grow in your garden, then use another flower that you consider to be beautiful or that has a pleasing scent. Some spells do relate to symbols of ancient traditions and these should never be mixed up, as this causes confusion to you and will cause the spell to fail.

Aries: The Ram

Using the powers of Aries, a symbol of leadership, this is a spell
for increasing assertiveness and self-confidence.

You will need

A red candle

A picture of a
ram

A red flower

A compass

•

A sheet of white
paper

•

A red pen

A Fire sign, Aries is bursting with dynamic energy.
This sign uses inspiration as a catalyst for change and
encourages forward movement. Ruled by the Ram, Aries
energy is aggressive and competitive, as well as exceedingly
confident. Use this spell if you lack the courage and
strength to get what you want.

Method

Take a red candle, a red flower (red is the colour dedicated
to Aries) and a picture of a ram and place them on a table.
Face the east and light the candle. Using a red pen, on a sheet
of white paper list the situations in which you wish you were
more assertive. When you are done, carefully fold the paper as
many times as you can and place it underneath the flower. Now
sit still with your eyes closed and imagine a warm red light
shining on you. See yourself becoming stronger-willed and
more assertive, yet not vicious or cruel. Know deep down
inside that you can be strong if you need to be. Pinch out the
candle, but leave the folded paper underneath the flower until
the flower has dried out completely. The next time you are
facing a difficult situation, recall the warmth of the red light.

Taurus: The Bull

A spell to open your eyes and help you appreciate the beauty that exists in your life.

You will need

Your favorite
objects

Pictures of the
people you love

Ribbons in your
favourite colours

A compass

Taurus rules the senses and thus this sign is associated with all forms of comfort and beauty. Before you begin this spell, it is best to think about exactly what you consider beauty to be, whether in people, works of art or the natural world; as the old saying goes, 'beauty is in the eye of the beholder'. If you look hard enough, you will find that there is beauty in all of the people, objects and events in your life, however ordinary they may seem. Here is a spell to open your eyes to this beauty and to help you appreciate it.

Method

Set out onto a table a collection of things that you love; you can include your favourite flowers, pictures of the people you love, your favourite objects—anything in your life that makes you happy. Also include a few ribbons in your favourite colours. Stand facing south, hold your hands over the objects, and say:

'May I have beauty before me.
May I have beauty behind me.
May I have beauty to my left hand and to my right hand.
May I have beauty all around me,
and may I walk in beauty through my whole life,
through this beautiful world.'

Tie three knots in each of the ribbons and carry them around with you. You will soon recognise and appreciate the beauty in all that surrounds you.

Gemini: The Twins

A spell for renewing communication with a
long-lost friend, relative or lover.

You will need

Mementos of the
person with
whom you wish
to communicate

•

A photograph of
yourself and one
of the person with
whom you wish
to communicate

•

An envelope
large enough to
hold photos

•

Orange ribbon

•

Adhesive tape

Gemini is ruled by Mercury, the planet of travel and
communication. This sign is concerned with ideas, change,
adaptability and personal communications. Gemini's
symbol is II, the Roman numeral for two. Accordingly, its
power may be used to reconnect two friends, relatives or
lovers who have lost touch with each other.

Method

Sit quietly and consider your relationship with the missing
person. Place mementos of the person around you and recall
when you last saw or spoke to each other. Place a photo of
yourself and one of the loved one face to face inside an
envelope and seal it shut. Bind the envelope with orange
ribbon, reciting:

'With ribbon I bind, this symbol to find my ____ (fill in
friend, relative or lover) from time gone by. Saying that he (or
she) shall remember me, and a message swiftly fly to unite us
from the Earth's ends, together by day or night. By phone or
e-mail, by swift fax or snail, he (or she) is ready to write.'

Tape the envelope to a window in your home, facing the
direction the long-lost person is in, and mentally send out your
address or phone number to them. Within two weeks, a
message—often via a strange route—will bring news of them.
Take down the envelope and unwind the ribbon to release the
spell, all the while thanking the power of Gemini.

Cancer: The Crab

A spell to create a tough shell to protect and
defend a vulnerable interior.

You will need

A small box
with a separate
lid

Aqua, blue, or
green paper
•
Glue
•
Scissors
•
A seashell
•
Silver string

Cancer is symbolised by a crab with a hard shell—tender
underneath, yet tough on the outside. Although people born
at this time are by nature soft-hearted, sensitive and
compassionate, they, like most of us, can at times benefit
from the ability to project an armour-plated exterior to the
world. When you are feeling vulnerable, this spell can help
you build a protective shell to nestle into until you feel
strong again.

Method

Take a small box with a separate lid and cover both parts
with green-, blue-, or aqua-coloured paper (symbolising the
water the crab comes from). Snip off a few strands of your hair,
place them and a seashell in the box, and put the lid on. Take
some silver string and wind it around the box while saying:

*'As I wind this string to bind, a box of protection making.
I will be strong as I go along, my heart is not for breaking.
Should I fear, in any year, this charm I shall remember,
and know its power, in every hour, from January to December.
Be it so!'*

Hide the box on top of a cupboard or some other high
place. You will soon find it much easier to cope with difficult
people and situations.

Leo: The Lion

A spell to give you confidence and to enhance your position in the eyes of others.

You will need

- Metallic gold paper
- Scissors
- A pen
- Six yellow flowers, such as marigolds, sunflowers, and yellow daisies
- A shallow bowl
- A gold chain
- Gold-coloured baubles
- A tea light

The ancient Greek god Heracles's first labour was to kill the Nemean lion, and the constellation Leo is said to honour the bravery of this battle. But despite the vigour and stamina attributed to this mythical lion, lions in the real world are known to be rather lazy, spending a lot of time eating, resting, playing or grooming themselves. This spell is for those who desire the positive 'lionlike' qualities, but are not keen on doing anything too strenuous to acquire them.

Method

Cut out a circle of metallic gold paper. Write your name on it and draw the symbol for the astrological sign Leo. Take the paper outdoors on a sunny day and place it where the Sun can shine upon it. Lay the petals of six yellow- or gold-coloured flowers outside to dry out in the Sun. When the petals are dry, place them in a shallow bowl with a gold chain, some gold-coloured baubles, and a tea light. Set the bowl on top of your golden circle and light the tea light. See the tea light's flame reflected on the golden objects and say:

'I shall shine, be strong as a lion, my way ahead is bright.
My heart is gold, its power unfolds to show my own true light.
May I shine, may I shine, may I shine, in everything I do.'

Place the golden circle on the floor underneath the head of your bed. Wear the chain whenever you are going to face a challenging situation and know that you will succeed.

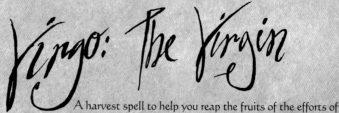

Virgo: The Virgin

A harvest spell to help you reap the fruits of the efforts of
the preceding months and to help you gather strength for the coming winter.

You will need

Fruits, grains,
seeds, berries,
flowers, twigs,
autumn leaves
(found, not
bought)

•

Symbols of
completed
projects, or of
those that you
wish to discard

•

Photos of your
family and
friends

•

Paper and a pen

•

A candle

•

String

The constellation Virgo is linked to Demeter, the Greek
goddess of the harvest. As in ancient times, today the
coming of winter is a good time for harvesting the rewards
of your achievements for the year and for discarding that
which is no longer necessary in your life. By harvesting the
fruits of your labour, you can gather the beneficial energies
that will sustain you for the rest of the year.

Method

Collect flowers, fruits, seeds, berries, twigs, leaves and anything
harvested from your own garden. Gather as well some symbols
of your work—in particular, anything that symbolises projects
that you have completed, or that you wish to discard. Finally,
gather some photos of your family and friends. On a warm
afternoon, set up a table and make a sacred space around it (see
pages 32-33), then set out all of the objects that you have
gathered. Burn any paper symbols of completed or discarded
projects using the flame of a candle, then say:

'Mother Nature, who has given me a bounty,
you who inspires my work, nourishes me, body and spirit,
I give thanks for all that you have granted me.
With these tokens I offer myself to protect the Earth.'

Tie the 'natural' symbols into a bundle with a string and hang it
on the branch of a tree. Place the photos where you can see
them at home or work, until Christmas time.

Libra: The Scales

A spell for balance, and to help you make the right decisions in your life.

You will need

Paper and pen

•

A small
pendulum (you
can make this
yourself by
suspending a
weight on a piece
of thin string)

•

A black candle
and a white
candle

•

An image of the
Scales of Justice

•

A compass

The constellation Libra is associated with balance and
justice. In our daily lives, we often have to juggle
conflicting demands on our time and energy and it can be
difficult to know how to balance these demands. When you
feel you need help prioritising the many obligations in
your life, use this spell to call upon the wisdom of Libra.

Method

Think about the demands on your time and write on a piece
of paper: 'Should I choose (choice A) or (choice B)?' Take a
small pendulum and hold it over your right palm. Ask it: 'Can
you show me a yes?' Note how it swings, then say: 'Can you
show me a no?' The pendulum will now swing differently.
Light a black and a white candle and place the paper between
them. Now place a picture of the Scales of Justice in front of
the paper. Holding your pendulum over the paper, say:

*'Power of the pendulum, answer me, should I select choice
A or B? Is it right to make my way along the path that
follows A? Would a better option be if I go along with B?'*

Then say: *'Is A the right path?'* If the pendulum signals that
the answer is no, then say: *'Is B the right path?'*

You must abide by the decision shown to you by the pendulum.
Stick the picture of the Scales of Justice on the eastern wall of
your bedroom and leave it there until the project is completed.

76

Scorpio: The Scorpion

A spell to summon forth the identity of your secret admirer.

You will need

Paper and a pen

Four candles of
your favourite color

•

A small mirror

A new silver ring

•

Your favourite
incense

Incense burner

At the heart of the Scorpio constellation is the bright red star Antares, which burns with an intense energy and corresponds to the purposeful and passionate nature of those who are born during this time. Here is a spell which utilises the passionate energy of Scorpio to uncover the identity of a secret admirer.

Method

On a piece of paper, write down what you understand true love to mean. Include details of what you want from a lover and what you are willing to give in return. Spend at least three days considering these questions, keeping your writing hidden.

When you have finished writing, set four candles of your favourite colour in a square. Place a small mirror in the centre of the square, and place a new silver ring upon the mirror (silver, the metal of the Moon, represents the emotions). Light the candles and your favourite incense and think about what you have written. Look into the mirror through the ring and say:

'Scorpion, power of love, send an image from above,
if there is one who truly loves me, let me now their picture see.
If this secret can't be told, let my love shine out like gold,
that a love may come, soon.'

The face of your secret admirer may now appear in the mirror. Whether or not it does, kiss the ring and slip it on your finger. Any secret admirers will soon make themselves known.

Sagittarius: The Archer

A charm enlisting the talents and skills of the Archer
to help bring success in sport.

You will need

*A photo of the
prize you seek*

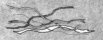

*Thread, wool or
thin ribbon in red,
blue, white, black
and green*

Five metal rings

Paper and a pen

*A small red
cloth pouch*

The symbol of Sagittarius is a mounted archer. Those born
at this time of the year are inclined towards a desire for
personal freedom, restlessness and a love of the outdoors.
They often have an interest in sports and enjoy both
solitary sporting activities and playing as part of a team.
Here is a charm calling upon the sporting prowess of
Sagittarius to bring success in a sporting endeavour.

Method

Decide which sport you wish to succeed at and to which
level you hope to aspire—skilled amateur or professional. All
levels will require dedication and practice, but a talisman can
give you an extra boost. Ideally you should dress in your
sporting costume while working this magic. Place a picture of
the prize you seek to win in front of you. Tie a different-
coloured thread to each of five metal rings, while saying:

*'May my dedication take me higher, to win the prize I so desire.
When the race is run so fast may I be nearer first not last.
Hard training will make me stronger, so I can go on much longer.
With my team I'll be a part, sharing my skills with all my heart.
As I strive to win the gold, sportsmanship I will uphold.'*

Repeat this mantra five times. Neatly write out a copy of the
spell and place it, along with the rings and the photo of the
prize you seek, in a red pouch. Keep the pouch near you
whenever you play the sport and your skill will improve.

Capricorn: The Goat

A garland spell for security and success in your career.

You will need

Holly, ivy,
spruce and other
available greenery

•

Florist's wire

•

Symbols of your
job

•

Green and dark
blue ribbons

•

Gold thread,
beads and tinsel

•

Real or chocolate
gold-coloured coins

•

Rose, cedar and
myrrh incense

In many ancient cultures, midwinter, or the winter solstice, was a time for celebrating the previous twelve months and for making plans for the coming year. With this spell, you build upon this tradition by making a garland that incorporates symbols of your achievements from the previous year to give you the strength and confidence you'll need to face challenges in the year to come.

Method

Begin by making a small garland of greenery, about 1 foot (30 cm) or less across, using holly, ivy, spruce—the plants dedicated to Capricorn—and any other greenery you can find. Bind it with florist's wire. Add symbols of your job to the garland, such as photos or small parts of projects you have finished. Take some green ribbon and wind it clockwise around the garland, then take some dark blue ribbon and wind it counter-clockwise around the garland, joining the ends in a bow. In the middle of the garland, hang strands of gold thread, coins, beads and tinsel. When your garland is complete, light a rose, a cedar and a myrrh incense stick and wave the garland through the smoke of each, picturing success and security at work in the year to come. Say:

'I ask for success and security, it is my will. So may it be.'

Hide the garland in a dark place, knowing it will bring you success in your career in the coming year.

Aquarius: The Water Carrier

A benevolent spell for helping people in need
and charitable causes.

You will need

A bottle of
spring water

A glass
container

A glass nugget
or marble

Some astrologers believe that the year 2000 marked the
movement of the vernal equinox to the constellation
Aquarius, thus we are on the cusp of the Age of Aquarius.
This age will last 2000 years, and many believe that it will
be characterised by peace and harmony. Aptly, the symbol
for Aquarius is a lone water bearer, pouring the waters of life
for others. With this spell, you can honour the benevolence
of Aquarius by helping others less fortunate than yourself
or by furthering a cause devoted to bettering the planet.

Method

Choose a project or charity that you wish to help. Go to a
nearby river and take with you a bottle of spring water, a glass
container and a glass nugget or marble. Stand beside the river,
holding the bottle in your hands and wish as hard as you can
that a solution to a desperate situation may be found. Pour half
of the bottle of spring water into the river, and say:

*'Every river connects to the sea, and every ocean connects to the
others. Rain drawn from the sea falls on the land. All people
are brothers. Let my intent travel around the whole world,
reaching those in greatest need.'*

Kiss the glass nugget or marble and throw it into the river. Pour
the rest of the spring water into the glass container and take it
home. Set it in a place where you will see it often and
remember your good wish for the world.

Pisces: The Fish

A spell to give you the strength to achieve your
most challenging aspirations and desires.

You will need

Stiff wire

*Pale blue, sea-
green, and silver
ribbons*

•

Gold-coloured paper

•

Scissors

•

*Small bells or wind
chimes*

•

Silver thread

•

Red ribbon

•

*Sweet-scented
incense sticks*

Pisces, the twelfth sign of the zodiac, is represented by two
fish swimming in opposite directions, bound together by a
line. This image represents a duality, the struggle of the
spiritual soul within the physical body. In the Chinese
tradition of Feng Shui, fish are often used to help stir up
energies where there is a dead place in a house. In this spell,
they are used to stir up energy and inspiration.

Method

Twist some stiff wire into a circle and tie pale blue, sea-green
and silver ribbons onto it. Cut out the shapes of two fish from
gold-coloured paper. Using silver thread, hang the fish and
some small bells or wind chimes to the mobile, so that they
swing freely. As you are creating this mobile, think of long-term
plans that need to be set in motion or about any aspirations or
desires which seem especially difficult to accomplish.

Make the mobile as beautiful as you can. Look at the bells,
ribbons and fish, and see each as a symbol of energy and
inspiration. With a red ribbon, hang the mobile in a corner of a
room where a draught can stir it, keeping the ribbons and fish
moving and allowing the bells or wind chimes to ring.

From time to time, light an incense stick and place it near the
mobile, so that the scent wafts in the same breeze. Each time
the mobile sways in the breeze, it will draw your hopes and
desires for the future closer.

Kitchen Witching

Everyone has a kitchen and in its cupboards and stores there are numerous useful items that can be used to bring luck, harmony and many other benefits to the magic worker. By carefully considering the luck you need and exploring the herbs, spices, dried fruits and kitchen implements at hand, you can enchant your life with the tastes and scents of delicious charms.

Magic From the Heart of the Home

This collection of magical spells uses common plants, herbs and spices that you may already have in your kitchen. If you grow these plants you can use fresh leaves or stems, but dried culinary herbs will work as well. Plants can be used as talismans and luck-bringers, in healing and soothing teas and to ward off harm.

A Spell Weaver's Storeroom

The kitchen is traditionally the heart of the house, where the daily benediction of preparing food takes place. It is where many of the original tools of the witch or spellmaker are to be found, including the *besom*, the old-fashioned broom made of birch bristles bound to a handle of sacred ash. The cups and bowls are all used in various forms of spells and charms, saucepans have replaced the cauldron in which potions are brewed and teapots make herbal tisanes. Spices, found in most kitchen cabinets, have particular attributes for bringing health and

*A traditional witch
and her broomstick*

wisdom, pleasure and protection to those who use them, in fact, most herbs and spices that are safe to eat, in appropriate portions, are safe to use in magic.

The Kitchen Tradition

In the past, many herbs and useful plants for dyeing and magical purposes would be grown or gathered from the wild, so a knowledge of the names and natures of these was very important. Much of this plant lore was handed down through families and in most communities there were men and women who possessed skills in using plants for medicine or herbs for healing. Later these people were called by other names, such as witches, wise women or cunning men. They kept the magical arts alive, drawing on inherited wisdom to preserve and expand their knowledge of useful materials.

When books began
to circulate, first as
hand-written manuscripts
and later as printed works, witches
expanded their knowledge using information
from other lands and earlier times.

As well as using plant magic they understood the power of the seasons, knowing when it would be best to perform any kind of magic, divination or healing. They observed everyone and everything that happened around them, from the opening of the first flower in spring to the migration of birds, the movements of clouds and the activities of their neighbours. All this could help them see into the future or give advice to those who asked. They worked closely with the powers of nature, with stones and twigs, pure water and dark skies studded with stars, where they saw what was to be. Much of this ancient knowledge has come down to us, but we can only get it to work if we carefully follow the rules, wishing harm to no one and seeking to change only ourselves.

Modern Day Magic

The following spells are based on tried and tested old arts, but they will work as well in the twenty-first century as they did in the twelfth, if those who seek to understand old magic treat it with respect and care. By carefully preparing for any spell, getting all the necessary items, the threads, spices, containers and so on ready before starting, and preparing yourself, you can draw on the great store of inherited wisdom and the vast power of the gods of nature, to help with your spells and bring you luck, just as your ancestors did, in days gone by.

The modern spell weaver's tools

91

Make a Mint

A traditional spell using the herb mint to ask for greater riches.

You will need

Green felt

•

*Green thread and
needle*

*Ten whole dried
mint leaves*

•

*Sky-blue paper
and pen*

•

Four gold candles

*Four coins of
different values*

Mint is a herb used in tea and cooking, but the word also describes the place where money is created. By using this herb in a spell, you may attract a small amount of cash to yourself. If you require money in order to buy an object or accomplish a task, a spell aimed at this end result may be more effective. However, if you just need a bit of extra cash to get you through the week, this spell can also help.

Method

Make a pouch of green felt (green symbolises both the money and the mint) and place ten dried mint leaves inside. On a sheet of sky-blue paper (to symbolise the riches that will materialise 'from the heavens'), write a sum of money, preferably less than £50. Place the pouch on a table with four gold candles, four coins of different values and the paper. Place one gold candle and one coin at each corner of a square and light the candles. Now sing, in any tune you like:

*'Lord of money, this I pray, that some cash will come my way.
I will work to earn the sum, if to me it now will come,
and by effort I shall pay for all the coins that come my way.
Please, please, please, send it soon.'*

Dance around the candles four times, then sit quietly, holding the mint pouch and consider whether a lottery win, a new job, or the payment of a debt owed to you would provide you with what you need. You may soon find yourself a bit wealthier.

Rosemary for Remembrance

A spell to open your mind to what has been forgotten.

You will need

*Four freshly
picked sprigs of
rosemary*

*Pale blue, dark
green, red, and
white embroidery
thread*

Green ribbon

Rosemary is a wonderful herb that can be used in cooking, as a soothing tea, or as incense (hence its old French name, *incensier*). Bees love the blue flowers, and the leaves keep stored clothes smelling sweet. Traditionally it was thought to help the brain and memory; in *Hamlet*, Shakespeare wrote 'There's Rosemary, that's for remembrance . . .', and sprigs were often carried at funerals. Here is a charm you can make using the power of rosemary to improve your memory.

Method

On a dry sunny day, pick four stems of rosemary, one by one, while saying:

'This twig I pick that I may remember all my deeds from May to December. This twig I gather that I may recall all of my friends in the spring or the fall. These rosemary leaves I gently take to recall good times with no mistake. This stem I pluck from the green rosemary that my love will not forget me.'

Place the tips of two stems one way and the other two the opposite way. Bind the bundle with threads of pale blue (for the flowers), dark green (for the leaves), red (for the stems), and white (for the underside of the leaves), so you end up with a cigar-shaped charm. Tie a green ribbon around the middle of the charm and hang it where you will see it every day. Every time you see the charm, you will be reminded of those things which you must not forget.

Sage for Wisdom ◎

A spell for summoning the power of sage to increase your wisdom.

You will need

Nine freshly picked stems of sage

The symbols of the four elements: a stone, a bowl of water, a red candle and incense

•

If you do not have a garden, a plant pot with earth in it

Sage has long been considered a healthful and magical herb. In the Middle Ages, there was a well-known saying: "If you would live forever and aye, eat some sage leaves every day." Traditionally, Native Americans used dried sage, bound into bundles and set smouldering, to purify their sacred spaces. But most of all, sage has long been known as the herb for wisdom. The Celts believed that if a bride carried sage, she became wise. Here is a spell to increase your ability to draw wisdom from life experience.

Method

Pick nine stems of sage before the herb has flowered, when the Moon is waxing. Set up an altar using the four elemental symbols from The Spirit of Sacred Space spell (see page 32). Place these symbols around the edge of the altar. In the centre of the altar, make a circle using the sage twigs, laying them all in the same direction. Light the candle and hold your hands over the ring of sage, trying to sense the energy from it. Sing:

'In magic circles of every age, when wind is calm or tempests rage, when magic sleeps or folly shows, from this ring of holy sage, let the power of wisdom flow.'

Pick up one leaf and chew it, imagining it awakening insight, common sense and wisdom within you. The other stems should be taken outside and planted in the ground, or in a plant pot. If they grow, wisdom will be yours for the rest of your life.

Take Back Thyme

As we all know, time
and tide wait for no man, so here is a spell to master time.

You will need

A pot of
growing thyme,
any variety

•

Silver foil

•

Paper and a pen

Sweet-scented
oils

Candles

Black marker

In today's hectic world, many people are hard-pressed to find the time to do everything that needs to be done. Indeed, we often find that our time is not our own. This spell will help you restore some spare time to your life by setting a pattern during a week-long magical rite.

Method

Choose a time frame of fifteen minutes every day when no one will disturb you. On day one of seven, take a pot of thyme and cover it with silver foil (symbolising mind power). Relax, breathing deeply for a few minutes. Make a list of the things you need time to do—these must be things just for you. Place the list under the thyme pot. On day two, take a bath with scented oils by candlelight and think about your list. Then add to the list and inspect the plant, watering it and giving it kind words. On day three, list things that waste your time. On day four, select a relaxing task from your first list and do it, stating:

'This is my time and be sure that I'm going to use it how I will. No other can my time slot fill.'

On day five, talk to your thyme plant, pouring out your complaints and delights. On day six, try something new that you have always wanted to try. On day seven, take the list of time-wasting items and cross out each one firmly with a black marker. Recognise that you can take back your life. Perform this ritual as often as needed for the rest of your life.

A Treasure Hunt

A household spell to clean up your kitchen and find a hidden treasure.

You will need

An old sheet

•

A messy drawer
or cupboard

 New
string

An upright
container, such as
a tall can or an
ice cream carton

An artificial
flower

•

Pretty wallpaper
or shelf paper

Nobody likes to do kitchen chores, but with imagination and some magic, they can be enjoyable. Here is a spell for tidying up and for revealing a hidden treasure at the same time. Several players can perform this spell together.

Method

Spread a sheet out on a flat surface. Empty out the contents of a messy drawer or cupboard onto the sheet, while singing:

'If I'm rich, or if I'm poor, I'll find treasure in this drawer. I will seek a hidden hoard within the maw of this cupboard. In my house are treasured friends, lost among life's odds and ends. In my search, both short and sweet, I'll find some gifts and leave it neat.'

Thread onto some string anything you can find with a ring or handle, then lay the threaded items in a circle on the sheet. Stand anything long in a tall container at the center of the circle. Everyone should add a verse about each item, such as:

'Here's a little silver spoon, I'll make it shine just like the Moon.'

Eventually, you will discover a long-lost trinket—the hidden treasure. Line the drawer or cupboard with paper, return the threaded items and fasten an artificial flower to the handle to show the magic you have worked. When you are done, say:

'I place my things quite tidily, the spell is done. So may it be!'

Sealed spell

Harmony in the Kitchen

A traditional spell to make your kitchen a relaxing,
peaceful gathering place for family and friends.

You will need

Wooden spoons

*Decorative
adornments such
as coloured
ribbons, artificial
flowers, glitter,
pictures and
photographs*

In ancient times, the task of cooking was done over a fire
at the centre of the main room in the family's living
space. Gradually, this important domestic task became
relegated to a special room set aside for food preparation,
away from the rest of the home. Today, the two traditions
are beginning to merge, and the kitchen is becoming the
heart of the home once again. Here is a spell to attract
peace, love and fun into the realm of the kitchen.

Method

By making your kitchen special to each person who uses it,
this room can become a centre for harmony and life. Let the
family decorate wooden spoons with anything they like, from
coloured ribbons and glitter to photographs, pictures,
coloured markers or anything else you fancy. While you are
all decorating the spoons, say, in unison:

*'Wooden spoons, hark to me, stir up peace and
harmony. Bring in joy and love and fun, through the
door, for everyone.'*

Affix the decorated spoons over your kitchen door to attract
love, peace and joy into this symbolic centre of the
household. Leave the kitchen and, one at a time, come back
in through the door above which the spoons are affixed.

Lucky Spices

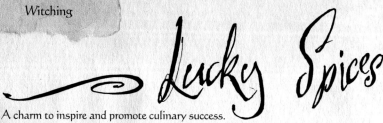

A charm to inspire and promote culinary success.

You will need

*A lime or other
small citrus fruit,
whole cloves, and
orrisroot powder*

•

*A large-mouthed
glass jar with a lid*

•

*A small spoon,
spices, recipe
pictures, and small
kitchen implements*

•

Dry white rice

•

Flour

•

A white candle

Although some cooks have to follow each step in a recipe book very carefully to be successful, there are some who just know intuitively how much salt, sugar or baking time a dish needs to be perfect, relying on luck and experience for results. Here is a cooking charm for achieving this kind of 'effortless' culinary success.

Method

Make a pomander by completely studding a lime or some other small citrus fruit with cloves and dipping it into orrisroot powder. Hang it up to dry completely. Place symbols of the kind of cookery you do into a glass jar—a small spoon, spices, pictures of your favourite dishes and small kitchen implements, for example. Use dry white rice to fill in the spaces. Place the dried pomander on top of this collection, to ward off disappointments. Put the lid on the jar and place the jar on your kitchen counter. Form a circle of flour around it, light a white candle, and say:

*'Jar of luck, to me please bring the flavour to my cooking.
When I give the jar a shake, bless the stew or bread or cake,
and when my friends come round to eat
may they find my dishes sweet,
whether I boil or roast or bake.'*

Pests Away

A spell to drive even the most persistent mouse from your home.

You will need

A picture of a
mouse

Camphor
or mothballs

Three black
candles

Lentils or any
other hard grain
that doesn't
appeal to mice

A straw
broom

Some witches claim to be able to talk to animals. Sometimes they ask them for help, and sometimes they try to persuade those that are a nuisance into going away. Typically, the language of the animal and the herbs and spices that the creatures dislike are used. Magic is often spoken as well, to make the spell extra effective. Here is a spell to help you get rid of even the most determined mouse.

Method

Get a picture of the type of mouse that is troubling you and some old-fashioned camphor or mothballs. Place the camphor or mothballs in a circle around the mouse picture. Light three black candles, set in a triangle around the circle of balls and pour a ring of lentils, or any other hard grain that doesn't appeal to mice, around the triangle. Sing, in any tune you wish:

'Mouse, mouse, leave my house, go from here quite quickly.
Tell your friends they'll meet swift ends, or end up very sickly.
From each room by power of broom I sweep you out so neatly.
I send you out, don't turn about, depart from here completely.
Go now, go now, go now!'

Throw the lentils outside your house, as far away as you can. Place a mothball at each point where the mouse has been spotted. Use a straw broom to sweep a symbolic magical circle around the edge of each room where the mouse has been seen, and rest assured that the offending creature will not return.

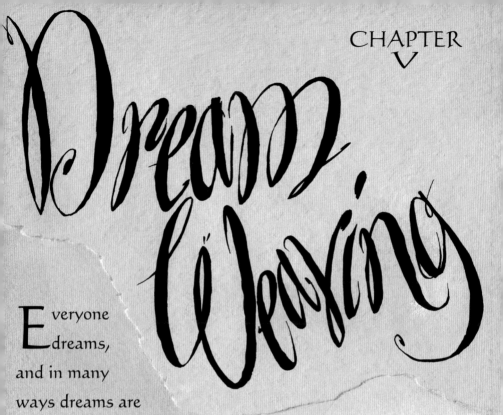

Dream Weaving

Everyone dreams, and in many ways dreams are the doorway to the magical layers of your inner mind. By learning to recall dreams, to understand and direct them, today's spell weavers can access huge areas of powerful information. You may have fascinating adventures that show your courage, unveil forgotten friendships, bring solutions to problems or see into the future. With practice you can control and direct these magical times and draw strength, inspiration and a sense of wonder from them.

Finding Insight in Dreams

Many of the images, transformations and
applications of magic happen in another dimension, sometimes called
the 'astral realm', so it is important that the spell caster finds ways to
access this place of vision. Everyone has the mental tools to reach into
this dimension within their subconscious or inner minds, but bringing
back clear memories and impressions requires practice.
The subconscious guards its secrets and magic workers have to find
the key that will unlock this hidden treasure chest of vision. The way
in is through the door of dreams, not just the spontaneous ones at
night, but daydreams, meditations and inner journeys can all help
make a clear and usable connection to these inner worlds.

The Dream Diary

Although some people don't remember their
dreams, everyone does dream during sleep.
One of the best ways of unlocking the door
of dreams and memories is by the use of a
dream diary. Any book will do, so long
as it is always to be found, with a
working pen, near the sleeper's
bed. Immediately on
waking, even in the
middle of the night, it
is essential to get into
the habit of writing
down memories,
impressions,

A dream diary

or just fleeting images from the dream, no
matter how vague. During the day other
fragments may come to you and should also
be jotted down. Gradually memories get
clearer and more detailed. Our dreams may
predict the future, or offer solutions to
problems, but unless they are
recalled in the morning, no use
can be made of this knowledge.

Deciphering Dreams

As well as showing aspects of another
dimension, our dreams reveal their
contents by use of images, symbols and
sometimes jokes. Although there are lots

of books that aim to explain the meanings of dream symbols, these are often personal. For example, a dream of a gift may be seen in terms of a spiritual gift, such as healing, or interpreted as a present, indicating that the dreamer should concentrate on the present time. Others might see the gift as a box containing a pleasant surprise or as a symbol of a protected place or even being boxed in.

Whatever the reading, dreams have to be recalled before they can be understood and the following spells will help you come to grips with these hidden aspects of your sleeping mind. Although catching hold of your dreams may seem very hard at first, it is well worth continuing to recall at least part of a dream each time you wake. Some people find using a Native American dream catcher can help. It may also help if you have a friend who you can talk to about your dreams, perhaps exchanging ideas and insights. Sometimes groups of friends find they are sharing symbols, characters or other aspects of action in their dreams. As you discover more you will also be discovering parts of the hidden side of you, where you may well have characteristics that you feel you lack in real life. If, in dreams, you can solve problems or overcome monsters, what is stopping you from doing the same when you are awake? Try and you might be surprised at your own power.

Dreaming While Awake

Magic also relies on waking dreams, induced through meditation, daydreaming and creative visualisation, for it is by these means we are able to talk to our inner selves, to receive guidance, help and inspiration. The spells in this chapter are aimed at awakening a clearer connection between waking and sleeping minds, so that dreams can be remembered and their contents used.

A dream catcher can help you capture your night-time ideas and insights.

111

Moon Sleep Spell

A spell to ensure that your dream memories stay
with you in your waking hours.

You will need

Paper and pen

•

*A piece of plain
cotton, about 20 x
10 inches
(50 x 25 cm)*

•

*White thread and
needle*

*Dried jasmine
flowers, hops, poppy
petals, rose petals
and lavender flowers*

•

*One black candle,
one white candle
and two silver
candles*

Sleep analysts believe that dreams encapsulate different aspects of our psyche and circumstances, including our life situations, relationships and experiences. If this is true, then an awareness of our dreams can help us to understand our thoughts and emotions. Unfortunately, we cannot always remember our dreams, thus hindering our abilities to learn from them. With the help of this spell, you can enhance your level of dream perception.

Method

Record your dreams from recent nights as best you can. Find out what phase the Moon was in each night—this tells you during which phases you best recall your dreams—and record this information as well. Sew a small pillow from cotton, about 10 x 5 inches (25 x 13 cm), and loosely fill it with dried flowers associated with the Moon (*see left*). On the evening of a new moon, light one black, one white and two silver candles to represent the Moon's phases: dark, new, waxing and waning. Place the dream pillow under your normal pillow and say this spell:

'Flowers of magic, flowers of sleep, let my moon-dream visions creep into my memory to keep. Show to me in bright day's light all the adventures of the night. So may it be.'

Note every dream you can recall—even fragments—for at least two months. You will find that your memory will begin to improve and that patterns in your dreams will start to emerge.

Nightmares Away

A spell to drive nightmares away and
return peace and restfulness to your slumber.

You will need

*A violet
or purple
candle*

*A copper coin
and a silver coin*

*A small
stone or pebble*

*A length of
white cord at
least 16 yards/
14½ metres long*

Nightmares or violent dreams happen to most people at
some time in their lives and can be very unpleasant. Many
people experience these unpleasant dreams when they are
under stress or going through a change in their life pattern.
This spell can be used to discourage nightmares and to
encourage a good night's sleep. It is best performed during
a waning moon.

Method

Light a violet candle—the colour violet helps attract the
power of the Moon. Put a copper coin on the floor under the
top left-hand corner of your bed, a silver coin under the top
right-hand corner and a small stone or pebble under the bed, in
the centre. Fasten one end of a length of white cord to the top
right-hand corner of the bed. Carefully wind the cord around
your bed, clockwise, so that it lies on the floor surrounding it.
As you do this, sing or say:

*'This cord I wind, all fears to bind, and from my dreams drive
out all nightmare scenes, all shouts and screams 'till daylight
shines about. So may this be!'*

Tie the end of the cord to wherever it finishes up, to complete
the circle. As you go to bed each night, mentally visualise the
objects around the bed and know they will bring calm and
safety, repeating the rhyme if necessary.

Sweet Dreams

A spell to summon those you are missing into your dreams.

You will need

A picture of those whom you miss

A silver picture frame

Small self-adhesive stars

If you recognise that the people you love who are far away from you can see the same sky, the same Moon and, unless they are in the other hemisphere of the world, the same star patterns as you, this can help you feel closer to them. Sending a spell for a star to shine on those you miss and to inspire a dream of them will also help bring them psychically closer to you.

Method

When it is dark outside, search the night sky for a star. If you can't actually see any, imagine one. Picture the faces, voices and presence of those you miss, laughing in the sky around the star. Imagine them seeing the star and noticing your face and voice too. Chant this spell to bring sweet dreams of those whose presence you miss:

"Starlight, star bright, bring sweet dreams to me tonight. Sweet heart, though we're apart, know you're always in my heart. Starlight and moonbeams, bring my lover in my dreams, so we can shine together, please. This will bring my sore soul ease."

Keep a picture of the person or people you miss in a silver frame and place it on the windowsill, so that starlight can fall on it and bring you sweet dreams of them. Stick a few self-adhesive stars on or around the picture every night, until you are together again.

Sealed spell ☞

Dreaming the Day Away

A daydreaming spell
to help you solve your problems and release stress.

You will need

Silver paper or
foil

Scissors

Ballpoint pen

Incense stick
with a relaxing
scent

In this modern, hectic world, our hurried lifestyle encourages the build-up of destructive chemicals in our system, which in turn can lead to illness or discomfort. This spell helps you to set aside a few minutes every day for daydreaming, to help you overcome stress and to guide you toward the solutions to your problems.

Method

Cut a circle out of silver paper (silver will attract the powers of the Moon) and lay it on a soft surface. Use a ballpoint pen to write your initials on the back of the paper in mirror writing, so that when you turn the circle over the letters stand out.

Light an incense stick and place your hands on each side of the circle. Focus on the most wonderful location you know—somewhere you have already visited or somewhere you wish to go. Let the image flood through you.

Become aware of a doorway or natural cave in the scene. Go towards it. Inside it will be light, together with a change of scene. This new scene will involve a problem you are trying to solve. As you look around, you will see clues to how the problem can be solved.

Allow your mind to drift over these clues, taking in possible solutions. After a few moments, bring your attention back to the present and note how relaxed and calm you are. Recall the details of the problem and its solution.

Web of Dreams

A magical charm to bring forth inner guidance while you sleep.

Native American in origin, dream catchers are typically made from a circle of thin twig wrapped in coloured threads with a net woven in the center. Their purpose is to catch positive dreams, while letting negative dreams pass through. Dream webs are made in a slightly different way and their purpose is different as well: they can induce a state of dreaming wherein inner guidance is discovered. Here is how to make a dream web.

You will need

Stiff cardboard (not corrugated)
8 inches (20 cm) wide

•

Scissors or a craft knife

•

Silver, blue, white, light green and pink thread, and a needle

•

Glitter powder or paint

•

Small, light ornaments such as beads, feathers or tassels

•

Cord

Method

Cut a circle out of stiff cardboard. Either leave it as a disk (*see right*) or cut out an inner circle so that you have a cardboard ring. With silver thread, sew across the circle, making spokes, as on a wheel. Secure a few coloured threads in the centre of the 'wheel' and wind each thread around each spoke in a clockwise spiral. Decorate the cardboard with glitter powder or paint and attach bright beads or other ornaments. As you make the web say:

'My dreams will be sweet and as I sleep, the powers of blessing will find me. My rest shall be calm, in slumber's arms, and troubles shall all fall behind me. So may this be.'

Plait a cord using the coloured threads and hang the web above the pillow of your bed. As you settle down to sleep, mentally trace the spirals of the web one at a time until you feel relaxed. Feel yourself float off into the starry realm of your dreams to receive the guidance that awaits you.

A Letter From Your Soul

A spell for communicating with those you have lost.

You will need

Eight candles,
either all white or
a mixture of
white, silver and
dark blue

•

Your favorite
coloured writing
paper and pen

Paints, glitter or
other decorative
materials

•

A fireproof
container, such as
a metal bucket or
deep tray

Often when someone close to us has died or moved away, we feel as if we never adequately expressed our love, wishes, thanks, regrets or even apologies to that person. Many magic workers believe in the law of karma, which entails accepting responsibility for all your actions, good and bad. If you have hurt people, mentally or physically, or if you feel that you never properly showed your love and affection, this can leave karmic debts. By writing a soul letter, you may be able to repay those debts.

Method

Think carefully about what you wish to say to the person you have lost. Light a row of eight candles, either all white or a mixture of white, silver, and dark blue (these are all soul colours). Take a sheet of paper in your favorite colour and write down everything you wish to say in the form of a letter. Be sure you are alone for this spell, and pour out your heart in the message, no matter how jumbled or repetitive it may be. You will probably feel very emotional, and writing your letter might make you cry. Take your time writing, decorating and finally signing the paper. When you are sure it is complete, carefully set fire to it in a fireproof container and watch it burn to ashes. Crush and sprinkle the ashes in the earth or into a river or let the wind carry them away from a high window. Know that your message will reach its recipient soon.

Dream Tea

A calming brew to help lull you to sleep and
to bring clear dreams.

You will need

1 tsp. dried
camomile flowers

•

½ tsp. dried
peppermint leaves

•

Powdered ginger

•

Powdered nutmeg

A bowl
and spoon

•

A strainer

•

Runny honey and
fresh lemon juice

•

A clean mug

Throughout history almost every culture has used herbs for
various purposes; every region had its helpful plants for
easing pain, cooling fevers, alleviating sickness and
encouraging sleep. Today, many of these plants are
commonly found in herbal and health food stores, so it is
safe for novices to use them in making their own
preparations. Always be sure you have the right herb for
your particular condition, though, and always buy from a
reputable source. Here is a safe, simple and effective brew
to help you sleep and to bring clear dreams.

Method

To make a cup of dream tea, put 1 tsp. of dried camomile
flowers, ½ tsp. of dried peppermint leaves, a pinch of
powdered ginger, and a pinch of powdered nutmeg into a
bowl. Add ½ pint (300 ml) of boiling water. Allow to infuse for
about five minutes, stirring it a few times and singing:

*'Sweet herbs, sleep herbs, mixed in this tea, fill me and thrill
me with bright dreams to see. Make it taste nice with flowers
and spice, and the addition of lemon and honey.'*

Strain the mixture into a clean mug. You can drink this brew
warm or cool, with lemon and honey added to taste. A small
amount will help sleep come to you sooner and will help
you dream more clearly.

Index

CREDITS

Quarto would like to
thank model Alicia Ryan
at BMA.
Arts and Crafts window
on pages 68 and 116
loaned by The Brooking
Architectural Museum
Trust, University of
Greenwich, Dartford
(a collection of
Architectural Details
1500 to the present day).
Tel: 020 8331 9897/
01483 274203